BOBBY, YOU SHINE BRIGHTER THAN ALL THE MAGIC IN THE WORLD. I LOVE YOU! - MOMMY

"SPEAK TO YOUR CHILDREN AS IF THEY ARE THE WISEST, KINDEST, MOST BEAUTIFUL AND MAGICAL HUMANS ON EARTH, FOR WHAT THEY BELIEVE IS WHAT THEY WILL BECOME" -BROOKE HAMPTON

Written By: Angela Lindsey
Illustrated By: Corryn Webb

978-1-7356169-0-2 Paperback
978-1-7356169-1-9 Ebook – Mobipocket
978-1-7356169-2-6 Hardback

For permission requests, contact AngelaLindsey@waverlythewitch.com
www.WaverlytheWitch.com

Publisher's Cataloging-in-Publication Data

Names: Lindsey, Angela, author. | Webb, Corryn, illustrator.
Title: Waverly the witch / written by Angela Lindsey; illustrated by Corryn Webb.
Description: Mechanicsville, MD: Angela Lindsey, 2020. | Summary: When Waverly's family moves to a new town, she feels nervous about starting school, but then she discovers her school is magic! Identifiers: LCCN: 9781735616902 |
ISBN: 978-1-7356169-2-6 (Hardcover) | 978-1-7356169-0-2 (pbk.) | 978-1-7356169-1-9 (ebook)
Subjects: LCSH Witches--Juvenile fiction. | School--Juvenile fiction. | Family--Juvenile fiction. |
CYAC Witches--Fiction. | School--Fiction. | Family--Fiction. |
BISAC JUVENILE FICTION / Fantasy & Magic | JUVENILE FICTION / School & Education

Classification: LCC PZ7.1.L5575 Wa 2020| DDC [E]--dc23

WAVERLY THE WITCH

WRITTEN BY
ANGELA LINDSEY

ILLUSTRATED BY
CORRYN WEBB

Waverly and her family are MOVING to a new house in a different town. TOMORROW is Waverly's first day at her NEW SCHOOL, and she is VERY nervous.

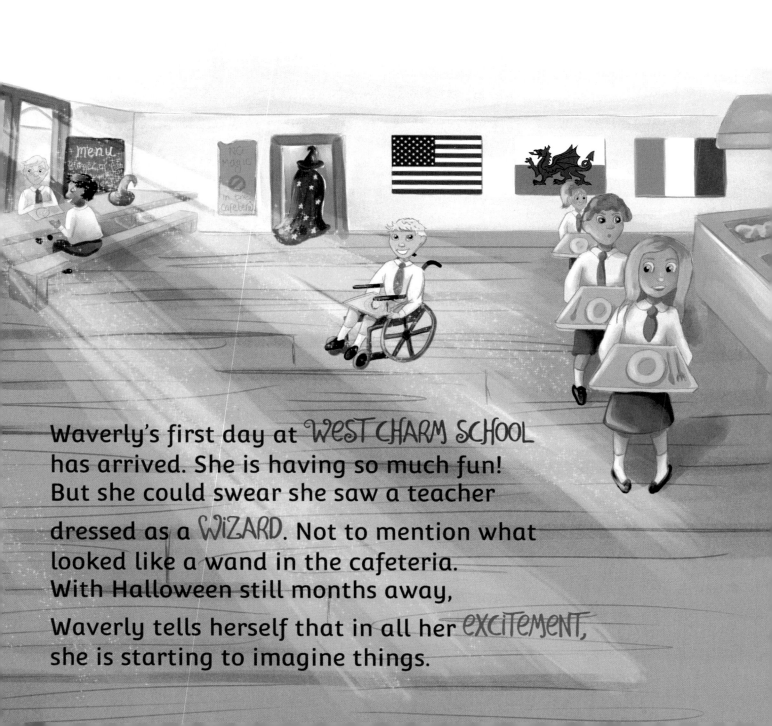

Waverly's first day at WEST CHARM SCHOOL
has arrived. She is having so much fun!
But she could swear she saw a teacher
dressed as a WIZARD. Not to mention what
looked like a wand in the cafeteria.
With Halloween still months away,
Waverly tells herself that in all her EXCITEMENT,
she is starting to imagine things.

Throughout the FIRST week, Waverly keeps noticing odd things. Once, she accidentally walked into a different CLASSROOM where it looked like everyone was making neon-colored potions in BUBBLING CAULDRONS! Even with all the strange things going on, Waverly is very HAPPY and quite comfortable at her new school.

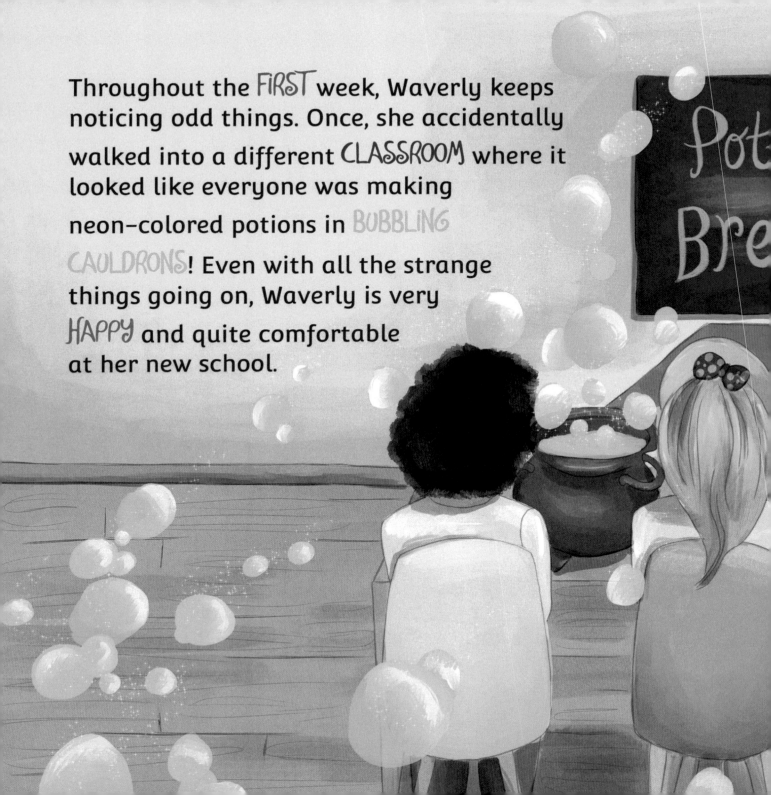

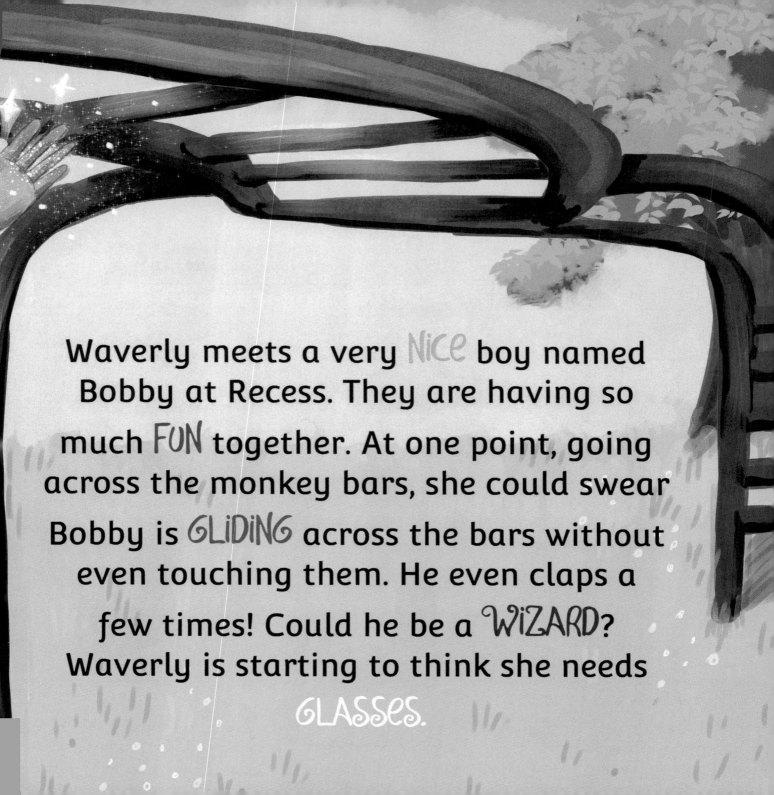

Waverly meets a very Nice boy named Bobby at Recess. They are having so much FUN together. At one point, going across the monkey bars, she could swear Bobby is GLIDING across the bars without even touching them. He even claps a few times! Could he be a WIZARD? Waverly is starting to think she needs GLASSES.

That night, during dinner, Waverly's parents ask her how SCHOOL is going. Waverly tells them how she met BOBBY and how they have so much fun together during recess.

She thinks he might be a WIZARD! She jokes that she might be attending a school for WITCHES. Her parents chuckle and shake their heads.

During her second week of SCHOOL, her suspicions come true! Waverly starts a new class called WITCHES 101, where she gets her very own WAND! Waverly is delighted! She really IS going to a MAGICAL SCHOOL.

That evening, Waverly excitedly tells her PARENTS all about her new class and shows them her WAND. They look at each other and tell her they are sure the teachers are JUST JOKING with her.

Waverly does very well in her MAGIC classes. Her teachers give her a FLYING BROOM as a reward. The broom is filled with ENCHANTMENT.

Waverly invites Bobby over to her house to PLAY
every weekend. He TEACHES her how to make new
POTIONS, and Waverly helps Bobby learn how
to ride his BROOM in her backyard.

Waverly keeps trying to tell her parents about MAGIC SCHOOL, but it seems like they don't believe her. She decides she will SURPRISE them with all the things she's LEARNED at the end of the year.

SCHOOL has become so thrilling for Waverly. She has learned how to cast so MANY SPELLS and make a dozen different POTIONS. Her teachers say she has an exceptional talent for MAGIC. Waverly and Bobby become quite the pair at WEST CHARM SCHOOL.

At the end of the year, Waverly graduates
with PERFECT GRADES.

After she and her parents get home from the CEREMONY, she asks if they can follow her to the BACKYARD. There, she jumps on her BROOMSTICK and effortlessly flies through the air. Her parents smile and are SO HAPPY.

Much to her SURPRISE, Waverly's parents take out their own BROOMSTICKS and start FLYING around with her. Waverly giggles with glee. Her parents are WITCHES TOO! They knew she was a WITCH all along! They just wanted her to FIGURE out who she was on her own.

ABOUT THE AUTHOR

Angela Lindsey is a talented author and an avid reader based in Mechanicsville, MD. A proud mom of one, Angela enjoys telling fun and inventive stories, taking inspiration from her son and the world around her. Angela is a successful businesswoman, owning two businesses and working in another family-owned company.

When she's not writing, Angela enjoys spending time at the beach, going on adventures with her family, and volunteering at the book fair at her son's school. She hopes to continue her writing journey, sharing many more stories with her young readers.

Made in the USA
Middletown, DE
24 October 2020